HORNED DINOSAURS

BY **'DINO' DON LESSEM**

ILLUSTRATIONS BY **JOHN BINDON**

LERNER BOOKS • LONDON • NEW YORK • MINNEAPOLIS

To Professor John McIntosh, a pioneer in the study of giant dinosaurs

First published in the United Kingdom in 2009 by
Lerner Books,
Dalton House,
60 Windsor Avenue,
London SW19 2RR

Website address: www.lernerbooks.co.uk

This edition was updated and edited for UK publication by Discovery Books Ltd.,
First Floor, 2 College Street, Ludlow, Shropshire SY8 1AN

Words in **bold type** are explained in the glossary on page 32.

British Library Cataloguing in Publication Data

Lessem, Don
   Horned dinosaurs. - 2nd ed. - (Meet the dinosaurs)
   1. Ceratopsidae - Juvenile literature 2. Dinosaurs -
   Defenses - Juvenile literature
   I. Title
   567.9'15

ISBN-13: 978 0 7613 4342 4

Printed in Singapore

TABLE OF CONTENTS

MEET THE HORNED DINOSAURS

WELCOME, DINOSAUR FANS!

I'm called 'Dino' Don because I love all kinds of dinosaurs. You've probably heard of some horned dinosaurs, such as *Triceratops*. What about *Torosaurus* or *Styracosaurus*? Here are the fast facts on some of the most amazing horned dinosaurs. I hope you'll have fun meeting them all.

CENTROSAURUS
Meaning of name: 'sharp-pointed lizard'
Length: 5 metres
Home: north-western North America
Time: 72 million years ago

PENTACERATOPS
Meaning of name: 'five-horned face'
Length: 8.5 metres
Home: south-western North America
Time: 70 million years ago

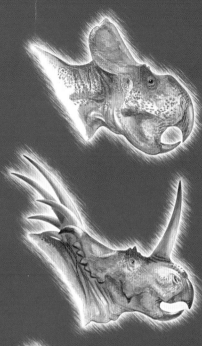

PROTOCERATOPS
Meaning of name: 'first horned face'
Length: 2.5 metres
Home: eastern Asia
Time: 80 million years ago

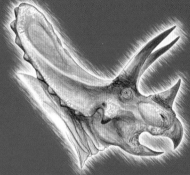

STYRACOSAURUS
Meaning of name: 'spear-spiked lizard'
Length: 5.5 metres
Home: western North America
Time: 73 million years ago

TOROSAURUS
Meaning of name: 'pierced lizard'
Length: at least 7 metres
Home: western North America
Time: 68 million years ago

TRICERATOPS
Meaning of name: 'three-horned face'
Length: 8 metres
Home: western North America
Time: 65 million years ago

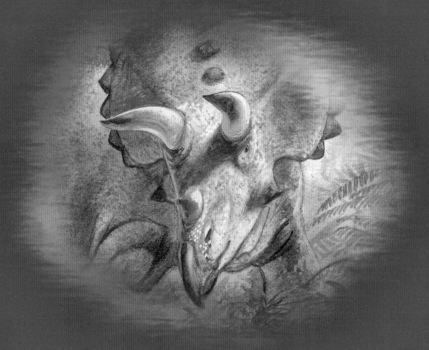

WHAT IS A HORNED DINOSAUR?

BANG! SCRAPE! Noises echo through the forest. Two male *Styracosaurus* are fighting. Each of these horned dinosaurs is as big as a tractor. They scrape horns and crash against each other's huge skulls.

The *Styracosaurus* aren't trying to kill each other. They're battling to show off to a female. Soon one will back off. The other will be the winner.

THE TIME OF THE HORNED DINOSAURS

Protoceratops

Centrosaurus

80 million
years ago

72 million
years ago

Styracosaurus and other dinosaurs lived on land millions of years ago. Scientists used to think that dinosaurs were reptiles. Some dinosaurs had scaly skin, like lizards and other reptiles do. Dinosaurs aren't reptiles, though. They were more closely related to birds than reptiles.

Pentaceratops

Torosaurus

Triceratops

70 million
years ago

68 million
years ago

65 million
years ago

Many kinds of dinosaurs had small horns.
The group we call horned dinosaurs had
the biggest horns of all. These dinosaurs
were **herbivores,** animals that eat plants.
Horned dinosaurs ate with a bony beak
called a **rostrum.**

DINOSAUR FOSSIL FINDS

The numbers on the map on page 11 show some of the places where people have found fossils of the dinosaurs in this book. You can match each number on the map to the name and picture of the dinosaurs on this page.

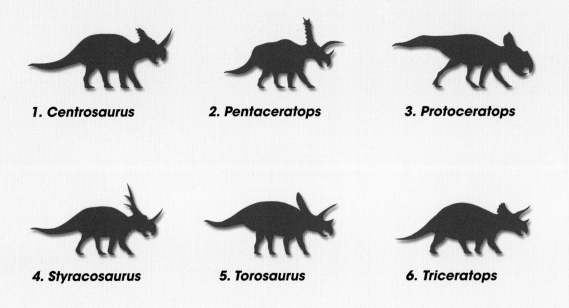

1. *Centrosaurus*

2. *Pentaceratops*

3. *Protoceratops*

4. *Styracosaurus*

5. *Torosaurus*

6. *Triceratops*

We know about horned dinosaurs from the traces they left behind, called **fossils.** Bones and footprints help scientists to learn how horned dinosaurs were built. However, fossils can't tell us what colour a dinosaur was or what its skin looked like.

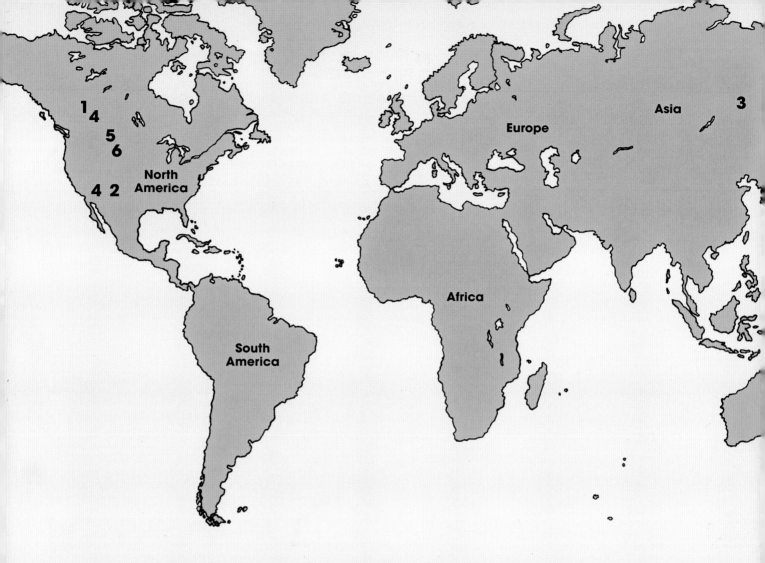

Dinosaurs lived in many parts of the world. However, people have found horned dinosaur fossils only in North America and Asia. As far as we know, horned dinosaurs only lived in these places.

HORNS AND FRILLS

Back off, *Tyrannosaurus rex!* *Triceratops* is the largest horned dinosaur. It's almost as long as a bus! This beast is showing off its horns to scare away the hungry *T rex.*

The sharp, bony horns of *Triceratops* were longer than a sword. They were probably too thin to hurt a *T rex* badly, but they may have scared away *T rex* and other **predators**, animals that hunt other animals for food.

Look at that huge frill! This ridge of bone grew from the back of a horned dinosaur's skull. Bumps and horns cover the frill of this male *Pentaceratops*. He shakes it so that the female will admire it and choose him as a mate.

A thick, bony frill may have protected a dinosaur from attack, but it was probably most useful in attracting a mate. The frill and head were covered with a material like that of a bird's beak. They may have been brightly coloured, like the beaks of some kinds of birds.

Two *Torosaurus* shake their big heads back and forth. They're trying to scare each other. Each dinosaur wants to become the leader of his **herd**, a group that lives and roams together.

Torosaurus may have been even bigger than *Triceratops.* Scientists haven't found a complete *Torosaurus* skeleton, but we know that its skull was as long as a tiger. That makes it the biggest skull of any animal that ever walked the Earth!

GROWING UP

These baby *Triceratops* have just hatched from their eggs. Their parents bring crushed plants to the nest. The adults put this soft food into the babies' mouths.

Scientists have never found fossils of baby
horned dinosaurs in a nest, but they think
that all dinosaurs probably hatched from
eggs, like birds do. Baby dinosaurs may
have been fed in the nest too.

The young *Triceratops* join their herd as
soon as they are big enough to walk. The
herd searches together for herbs and other
plants that grow near the ground. Each
dinosaur slices its food with small teeth and
a sharp, beak-shaped rostrum.

The young *Triceratops* grow larger horns as time passes. Males probably grew larger horns than females. Males needed big horns to attract mates.

One day, a pair of fierce *Albertosaurus*
attacks the herd. The adult *Triceratops* form
a circle, their huge heads facing outwards.
The predators pace back and forth, looking
for a safe place to attack. Finally, they
give up. The herd moves on.

Did horned dinosaurs really form circles to keep their herds safe? We don't know for certain. Some modern horned animals do.

HORNED DINOSAUR
DISCOVERIES

In 1923, scientists found a nest of fossilized dinosaur eggs. It was near the bones of many *Protoceratops*. The scientists thought the eggs were *Protoceratops* eggs. A fossil of another dinosaur lay nearby. Was it raiding the nest? The scientists called it *Oviraptor*. This name means 'egg thief'.

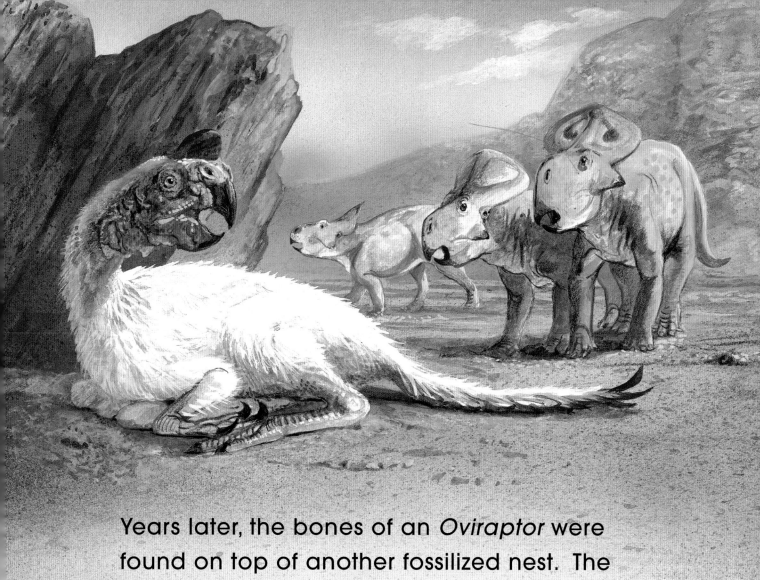

Years later, the bones of an *Oviraptor* were found on top of another fossilized nest. The eggs looked the same as those in the first nest. One egg held a fossil of a baby *Oviraptor*. The first *Oviraptor* hadn't been stealing horned dinosaur eggs after all. It had been guarding its own nest!

Fossils have also taught us how horned dinosaurs died. This huge herd of *Centrosaurus* was crossing a river when heavy rains caused a flood. The dinosaurs panicked. Some drowned. Others were crushed in the rush to get to dry land.

How do we know this disaster happened? Scientists found hundreds of *Centrosaurus* fossils buried in rocks in western Canada. The rocks were made of the kind of sand found on the bottom of a river. So these dinosaurs must have died in a river.

Predators ended the lives of many horned
dinosaurs. This *Velociraptor* attacks a
Protoceratops with claws as sharp as razors.
Who will win the battle?

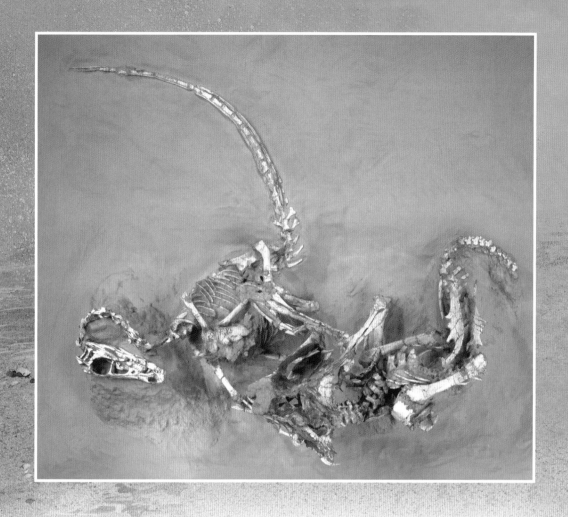

Both dinosaurs lost. Scientists found their skeletons buried in sand. A sandstorm may have covered them as they fought, or a sandy hill may have collapsed on them. Their skeletons slowly turned into rock.

The last horned dinosaurs died out 65 million years ago. Scientists think that's when a huge **asteroid** struck the Earth. The asteroid may have sent clouds of dust into the air. The dust would have changed the weather, killing plants and animals.

The asteroid crash may have been one reason that the horned dinosaurs died out. They are gone forever, but they left behind many traces of their lives. These fossils have shown us many things about the lives of the amazing animals we call horned dinosaurs.

GLOSSARY

asteroid: a large rock that moves in space

fossils: the bones, tracks or traces of something that lived long ago

herbivores: animals that eat plants

herd: a group of animals that live, eat and travel together

predators: animals that hunt and eat other animals

rostrum: a bony beak

INDEX

Text copyright © 2005 by Dino Don, Inc.
Illustrations copyright © 2005 by John Bindon
First published in the United States of America in 2005
Photographs courtesy of: © Royal Tyrrell Museum/Alberta Community
Development, p 27; © Denis Finnin, American Museum of Natural History, p 29.